ISE

PUBLISHING COMPANY

A WORD FROM OUR DOCTOR . . .

Let's be honest … ALL of us, at some time in our lives have wished we were just invisible. But sometimes, too much of a good thing turns out to be not so good after all.

Being invisible is one of those things. If you are the twin of a person with special needs - like a really cool brother with Down syndrome – you can become invisible just like the sun does during an eclipse. That does not always feel good. We try to always teach that we should not be defined by their disabilities but wait!!!

What if your life becomes defined by your brother or sister's disability and you lose your special identity. In other words, you become invisible. Samuel has written a book about his family experiences and he has beautifully expressed his feelings about life with a twin who takes a little more of his parents' time, gets a little more attention and is just more "visible". I think this is an important book for siblings to read and to understand.

With understanding and knowledge, love grows and frustration and the feeling that your voice is too small to be heard will become less important. After all, this is about being INDIVISIBLE with your siblings, not being invisible and apart. Good Job Samuel! You get it.

Michael J. Allshouse, DO, FACS, FAAP
Medical Director, Pediatric Surgery and
Pediatric Trauma Program
Valley Children's Hospital

The story "Am I Invisible?" Is an imprint of ISE Publishing Company
Published by: ISE Publishing Company
1620 W. Fairmont Ave,
Fresno, CA 93705-0323
Copyright © 2016 Jami Hamel De La Cerda, Samuel De La Cerda, & Diamond Learning Center
Fresno, California
All rights reserved.
Printed in United States
10 9 8 7 6 5 4 3 2 1

Library of Congress Control Number: 2016902492
Jami Hamel De La Cerda
The story of "Am I Invisible?" As told by Samuel John De La Cerda
Illustrated by Ernie "Hergie" Hergenroeder
Contributions by Kathy Eide Casas
Summary: "Am I Invisible?", Is a story of twin brothers, finding their individual voices and realizing every child is born to shine - wrapped up in an inspirational message of celebrating our differences.
ISBN: 978-0-9972135-0-8 (Hardcover)
Copyright to include all characters, design, story concept & text.

AM I INVISIBLE?

By: Samuel John De La Cerda

Illustrated by: Ernie **"HERGIE"** Hergenroeder

Samuel John De La Cerda
and his wonder dog Bella.

Have you ever felt invisible?
Felt like no one sees you standing in the room.
No one hears your voice or sees your bright smile.
Well, you are not alone. Samuel was one of those
children, and A LOT of others feel invisible at
different times and situations in their lives.
Having a sibling or even a twin is like having
a built in cheer team. But sometimes it is a challenge
to hear the cheer. There is no other light that shines
brighter than a child's light who feels loved, supported,
and embraced.

Samuel, thank you for sharing yourself.
You have found your voice and bright light,
and you have created an amazing opportunity
to inspire other children to love themselves,
to hear their cheer and shine ever so bright.

 Love you, MOM

**All children are Born to Shine
Enjoy Samuel's journey**

*Jami Hamel De La Cerda, M.S. SpEd
Founder/Education Specialist/ CEO Diamond Learning Center, Inc.
Adjunct faculty member CSUF in the Kremen School of Education and Human Development
Department of Literacy, Early, Bilingual and Special Education*

Our mother calls us her Three Kings. My oldest brother, "Isaiah" and my twin brother, "Elijah." My name is Samuel. Even though Elijah and I are twins, we look different because he has Down syndrome and is always the star attraction. That is why I feel invisible. This is my story . . .

Have you ever felt INVISIBLE?
I can see me, I can hear me, **BUT**. . . it feels
like everyone sees right through me.
They look right past me like I'm not even here!

Where's Sam? Is Sam here?
Sam, **SAM!**
Come Out, Come Out,
wherever you are. . .

I'm right here **GUYS!**

6

I will tell you a secret. Sometimes even grown ups can feel like they are invisible.

My teacher told me she once stood in front of her classroom while all her students kept talking and ignoring her. She felt so invisible that they couldn't even see her! She was their teacher and she really felt invisible.

"I'M RIGHT HERE STUDENTS!"

I told her, sometimes it helps me when
I talk with my very best friend . . .

Have you ever had a best friend who
loves you all the time?
Bella loves me even if she does have four
legs, a tail, and a big red, wet tongue.

She loves me even when I'm not nice.
She thinks I'm perfect no matter what!
I can always count on Bella.

I always shine bright with Bella. I can talk to her and she will always listen. She always sees me and understands me. I know that she loves me no matter what I do.

Bella has my back and she knows I'm right here!

Then there are my brothers... sometimes, I even feel invisible with them. Even when I do my best, it's hard to compete with them. If you have a brother or sister or maybe both . . .
Then you will know what I mean.

Sometimes it's twice as hard because I have a twin.
I am a twin, I am part of two, but still one.

We don't look alike,
and we don't even
sound alike, but Elijah
is my twin brother!

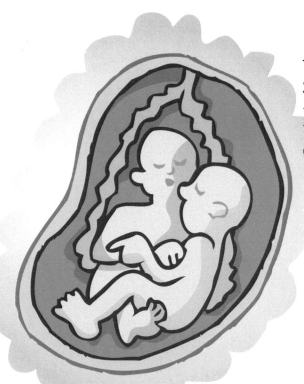

As twins, when we were very small, we shared everything. From the crowded space in our mommy's tummy . . .

To cuddle time in our daddy's arms.

We shared toys, strollers, blankets and more.

Now that we are bigger, we share different things . . . Games, toys, books, backpacks, shirts and shoes.

UGH! Sometimes I don't want to share. I just want my own Stuff!

13

We are the same, but completely different inside and out. Elijah has something special that makes him stand out . . .
Something EXTRA special! He has an extra Chromosome. Elijah has Down syndrome.

Do you know anyone who is **EXTRA special?**

People notice us, not for being the
same, but for being different . . .
He's so Cute? He's so special?
He's has Down syndrome? He's a star?

When people are born with Down syndrome
they look a little bit different . . .
and PEOPLE NOTICE DIFFERENT!

SHEESH!

Give me a break! Aren't I Cute? Aren't I special?
Aren't I brave? Aren't I a star?

Sometimes I get
FRUSTRATED and wish
that I could be somebody
different like Elijah.

CRASH!

But then, just as fast as I wish for that,
I'm Glad I'm ME!
I'm extra glad to be his big brother,
even if I am only one minute older.

18

Have you ever wished on a star?
What would you wish for?
Sometimes I wish I could be a king like Elijah,
then everyone would notice me too.

BUT WAIT!
Mom calls all of us boys her
"THREE KINGS"
So that makes me feel like a KING too!

I'm going to share something that I've learned. . .
Down syndrome is part of both me and my
brother Elijah. It is more of a challenge for him
then it is me. Life has more obstacles for Elijah.
Sometimes it feels like we're in competition, . . .
But we really are not!

My role as Elijah's
older twin brother
is to be an
AWESOME brother,
and his biggest fan,
and his best friend.

Sometimes Elijah needs help communicating and I am the only one that understands him. Sometimes I feel like I'm his BELLA. Mom says we share a special language that nobody else understands. Helping him makes me feel good and I like to SHINE for him.

I WANT TO BE HIS HERO!

I want Elijah to believe. . .
"Sam listens to me, he understands me,
and he loves me no matter what!"

We are not invisible!
We are born to Shine!

A WORD FROM OUR DOCTORS . . .

'Elijah is a delightful young boy. He has a terrific and positive attitude towards the many (frequently painful) demands on him for his various medical conditions.
This is a heartwarming and touching perspective from his brother, Samuel.'

Dr. Swati Banerjee
Pediatric endocrinologist
Valley Children's Hospital

Each child is a unique individual with unique abilities. Family dynamics are unique within each family. Yet, oftentimes within families, one child may excel or display different characteristics, leaving another child feeling overlooked and indeed, even invisible at times. In other situations, one child may feel that they don't get enough time or attention from a parent, because another sibling may require extra time and even more attention from a parent. Each family fits together like a puzzle.
Sam's book demonstrates that it is those very pieces that interweave and become the foundation for the commonalities shared. Thank you Sam for sharing your story with children everywhere; no matter what they look like or sound like or where they live. Remember...it is our differences that bind us together and make us stronger.

John Goodfellow
Occupational Therapist Registered

This believable story, told through Sam's eyes with accompanying charming illustrations, will be especially welcomed by families of children with disabilities. The issues described by Sam are not at all exclusive to siblings of children with Down syndrome.
The "invisible" child phenomenon is all too common in families where a disabled child requires the parents' disproportionate energy and care. Siblings will feel "heard" after reading this book and the parents will enjoy Sam's insights as well.
An excellent book recommendation for families on this important, often neglected, topic.

Cynthia J Curry
Director Genetic Medicine- Community Regional Medical Center, Fresno, Ca
Professor of Pediatrics Emerita, UCSF. Adjunct Professor of Pediatrics, Stanford.

Twins share an extremely close relationship with one another. This bond is undeniable, given that twins are uniquely paired with one another from the point of conception. From the first prenatal visits, it was understood that this would not be the usual twin journey.
One extra chromosome created an immense disparity between them focusing immediate priority to Elijah. Extra deliberation during office visits, referrals to specialist and the unexpected fame at an early age granted to Elijah were deafening.
Sam's journey with his twin brother is unique. Sam is a quiet, beautiful young boy with a radiant smile, He is bright yet overshadowed by events beyond his understanding or control. Now, it's Sam's turn to shine!

Raymond Miranda MD
Central Valley Pediatrics